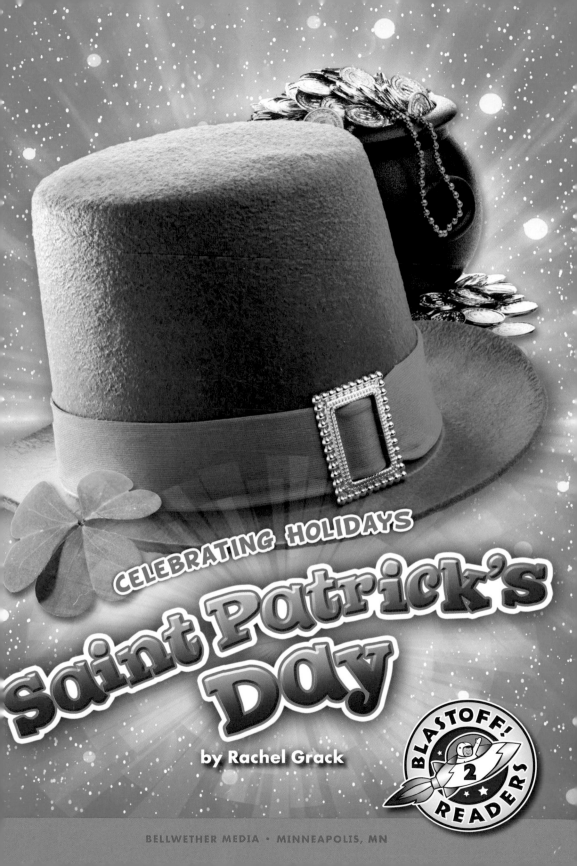

CELEBRATING HOLIDAYS

Saint Patrick's Day

by Rachel Grack

BLASTOFF! READERS 2

BELLWETHER MEDIA • MINNEAPOLIS, MN

Note to Librarians, Teachers, and Parents:

Blastoff! Readers are carefully developed by literacy experts and combine standards-based content with developmentally appropriate text.

Level 1 provides the most support through repetition of high-frequency words, light text, predictable sentence patterns, and strong visual support.

Level 2 offers early readers a bit more challenge through varied simple sentences, increased text load, and less repetition of high-frequency words.

Level 3 advances early-fluent readers toward fluency through increased text and concept load, less reliance on visuals, longer sentences, and more literary language.

Level 4 builds reading stamina by providing more text per page, increased use of punctuation, greater variation in sentence patterns, and increasingly challenging vocabulary.

Level 5 encourages children to move from "learning to read" to "reading to learn" by providing even more text, varied writing styles, and less familiar topics.

Whichever book is right for your reader, Blastoff! Readers are the perfect books to build confidence and encourage a love of reading that will last a lifetime!

This edition first published in 2018 by Bellwether Media, Inc.

No part of this publication may be reproduced in whole or in part without written permission of the publisher. For information regarding permission, write to Bellwether Media, Inc., Attention: Permissions Department, 5357 Penn Avenue South, Minneapolis, MN 55419.

Library of Congress Cataloging-in-Publication Data

Names: Koestler-Grack, Rachel A., 1973- author.
Title: Saint Patrick's Day / by Rachel Grack.
Description: Minneapolis, MN : Bellwether Media, Inc., 2018. | Series:
   Blastoff! Readers: Celebrating Holidays | Includes bibliographical
   references and index. | Audience: Grades K-3. | Audience: Ages 5-8.
Identifiers: LCCN 2016052741 (print) | LCCN 2016054065 (ebook) | ISBN
   9781626176232 (hardcover : alk. paper) | ISBN 9781681033532 (ebook)
Subjects: LCSH: Saint Patrick's Day–Juvenile literature.
Classification: LCC GT4995.P3 K64 2018 (print) | LCC GT4995.P3 (ebook) | DDC
   394.262–dc23
LC record available at https://lccn.loc.gov/2016052741

Editor: Christina Leighton   Designer: Lois Stanfield

Printed in the United States of America, North Mankato, MN.

Table of Contents

Saint Patrick's Day Is Here!

People are dressed in green. Some wear hats and **shamrocks**.

Others wave Ireland's flag.
It is Saint Patrick's Day!

What Is Saint Patrick's Day?

Saint Patrick figure, London parade

This holiday honors a **missionary** named Saint Patrick. He is the **patron saint** of Ireland.

People also celebrate Irish **culture** on this day.

How Do You Say?

English	Irish	Pronunciation
cheers	sláinte	SLAWN-cha
Happy Saint Patrick's Day	Lá Fhéile Pádraig Sona Duit	law AY-la PAWD-rig SO-na dit
holiday	lá saoire	law SEE-ra
Ireland	Éire	AIR-uh
shamrock	seamróg	SHAM-rohg

Who Celebrates Saint Patrick's Day?

Saint Patrick's Day is a **national** holiday in Ireland.

Ireland

Ireland

Other countries also honor this day. Canada and the United States have big celebrations.

Saint Patrick's Day Beginnings

Saint Patrick's Cathedral in Dublin, Ireland

Saint Patrick was born in Great Britain. He was kidnapped and forced to work in Ireland.

He escaped but later returned around the year 433 to spread **Christianity**.

Saint Patrick

Saint Patrick's Day started as a **religious** holiday. It has been celebrated in Ireland since 1631.

Saint Patrick's Day mass

Saint Patrick's
Cathedral
in New York City

Irish **immigrants** brought the
holiday to the United States.

13

Saint Patrick's Day falls on March 17. Many people believe Saint Patrick died on this day.

They honor him and
celebrate the Irish.

Saint Patrick's Day Traditions!

Many families have feasts. Corned beef, cabbage, and soda bread are favorite foods. Some people drop a shamrock in their drinks!

shamrock coffee

corned beef and cabbage

Irish Soda Bread

Have an adult help you make this bread.

Recipe

What You Need:
- 1 tablespoon butter
- 4 cups flour
- ½ cup extra flour
- 4 tablespoons white sugar
- 1 teaspoon baking soda
- 1 tablespoon baking powder
- ½ teaspoon salt
- ½ cup soft butter
- 1 cup buttermilk
- 1 egg
- baking sheet
- large mixing bowl and spoon
- measuring cups and spoons
- cutting board and knife

What You Do:
1. Preheat oven to 375 degrees Fahrenheit.
2. Grease baking sheet with butter.
3. Mix flour, sugar, salt, soft butter, baking soda, and baking powder in bowl.
4. Stir in buttermilk and egg.
5. Sprinkle extra flour over cutting board.
6. Lightly knead dough on cutting board and make round. Place on baking sheet.
7. Carefully cut an X across the top of the loaf.
8. Bake for 45 minutes. Serve warm.

Irish dancers in Saint Patrick's Day parade

People may go to church. They also enjoy parades and parties.

Irish bands play lively music for large crowds of people.

Green is everywhere on March 17. Some cities dye rivers green.

Chicago River in Illinois

People dress up as **leprechauns** and wear shamrock pins. They enjoy Saint Patrick's Day!

Glossary

Christianity—a religion based on the teachings of Jesus Christ and the Christian Bible

culture—the traditions and way of life of a group of people

immigrants—people who come from one country to live in another

leprechauns—small, elfish creatures from old Irish stories

missionary—someone who goes to another country to teach a religion

national—related to the entire country

patron saint—a saint who watches over a person or place

religious—having to do with a certain faith

shamrocks—small, green plants with three leaves; the shamrock is a symbol of Ireland.

To Learn More

AT THE LIBRARY
Keogh, Josie. *St. Patrick's Day.* New York, N.Y.: PowerKids Press, 2013.

Sebra, Richard. *It's St. Patrick's Day!* Minneapolis, Minn.: Lerner Publications, 2016.

York, M.J. *Celebrating St. Patrick's Day.* Mankato, Minn.: Child's World, 2017.

ON THE WEB
Learning more about Saint Patrick's Day is as easy as 1, 2, 3.

1. Go to www.factsurfer.com.

2. Enter "Saint Patrick's Day" into the search box.

3. Click the "Surf" button and you will see a list of related web sites.

With factsurfer.com, finding more information is just a click away.

Index